Let Heaven and Nature Swing

10 Songs for a Swingin' Christmas

Arranged by Don Marsh

PRODUCTS AVAILABLE

Choral Book 0-6330-1668-3

Listening Cassette 0-6330-1669-1

Listening CD 0-6330-1670-5

Accompaniment Cassette 0-6330-1671-3

(Side A: Split-track/Side B: Instruments only)

Accompaniment CD 0-6330-1672-1

(Split-track)

Cassette Promo Pak 0-6330-1673-X

CD Promo Pak 0-6330-1674-8

Instrumental Charts 0-6330-1837-6

INSTRUMENTATION INCLUDES

Alto Sax, Tenor Sax, Baritone Sax,

Trumpet 1-2, Trumpet 3-4, Trombone 1-2, Trombone 3-4,

Percussion, Rhythm (Keyboard, Guitar, Bass, Drums)

**ST. ANDREWS UMC
MUSIC DEPARTMENT
2045 S.E. GREEN OAKS
ARLINGTON, TX 76018**

GENEVOX

Let Heaven and Nature Swing
Foreword

Every Christmas I love to get out my favorite albums and hear the different ways Christmas carols can be arranged. Sometimes I want to hear the traditional "Drummer Boy" by the Harry Simeon Chorale, or "White Christmas" by Bing Crosby. But then I get out my Andy Williams Christmas album and remember the great swing feel to the original, "It's the Most Wonderful Time of the Year." The swing interpretations of Christmas favorites by such groups as Manhattan Transfer and Take Six have inspired me to do this collection of all swing styles, called *Let Heaven and Nature Swing*.

I've had a great time taking my favorite swing sounds, many of which you hear in commercials today, like Chips Ahoy ("Sing, Sing, Sing"), the Gap commercial, and others. The folks at LifeWay had thought that this book would appeal to "swingin' " student choirs who are into ska, The W's, and The Supertones, or the music of Swing Kids. But now we suspect that there are a lot of other groups who will want to include this music in their Christmas concerts, Living Christmas Trees, Christmas dinner theater presentations, and so forth. I just know that somewhere this Christmas a trio of girls in army uniforms will be singing the arrangement of "Angels We Have Heard on High (From Company C)" with a swingin' choir backup and a hot big band (charts are available).

In closing, I'd like to present this challenge to anyone: Play through the entire demo recording of "God Rest Ye Merry, Gentlemen" without tapping your foot or snapping your fingers in a hip swing style. If you can do that, this collection is not for you!

Enjoy!

Don Marsh

Contents

God Rest Ye Merry, Gentlemen

Traditional English Carol
Additional lyrics by
Don and Lorie Marsh

Traditional English Carol
Arranged by Don Marsh

O Come, All Ye Faithful

Latin Hymn
Ascribed to John Francis Wade
Tr. by Frederick Oakeley

JOHN FRANCIS WADE
Arranged by Don Marsh

Messiah Medley

with
And the Glory of the Lord
For unto Us a Child Is Born
Hallelujah Chorus

Bright gospel swing (♩ = ca. 100)

Arranged by Don Marsh

†"And the Glory of the Lord"

Opt. Altos join guys

† Words Isaiah 40:5; Music by GEORGE FREDERICK HANDEL.

46

spo - ken it. _____

C⁷   G¹³ F¹³/G G¹³   E₇#9   D₇#9

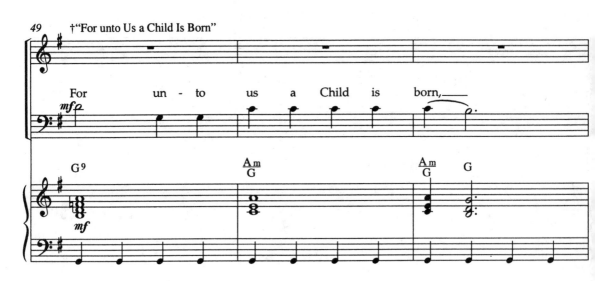

49   †"For unto Us a Child Is Born"

For   un - to   us   a   Child   is   born, _____

mf

G⁹   Am/G   Am/G   G

mf

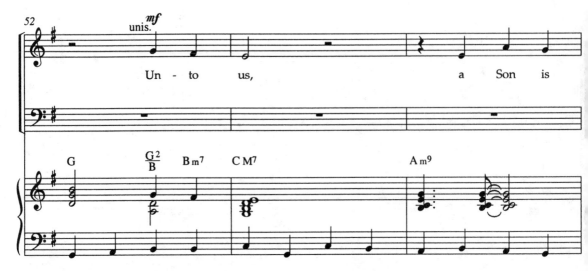

52   *mf*
unis.

Un - to   us,   a   Son   is

G   G²/B   Bm⁷   CM⁷   Am⁹

† Words Isaiah 9:6; Music by GEORGE FREDERICK HANDEL.

34

† Words Isaiah 19:6; 11:15; 19:16 (revised); Music by GEORGE FREDERICK HANDEL.

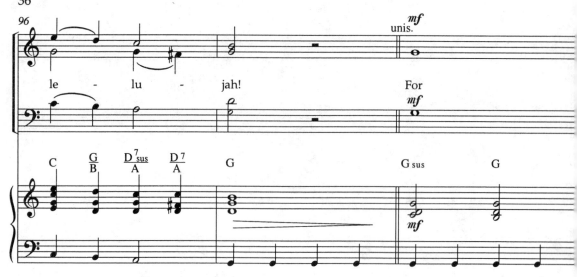

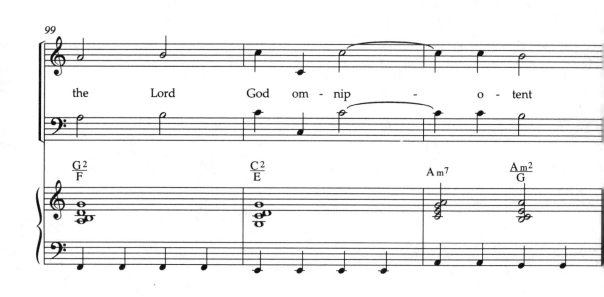

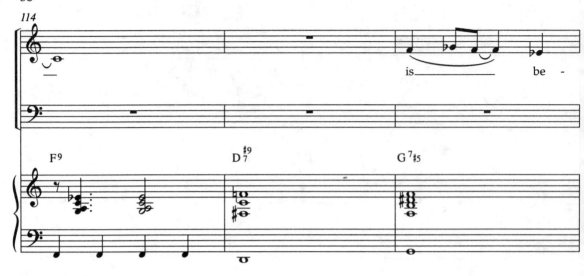

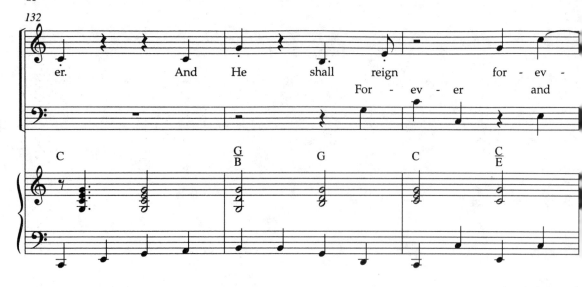

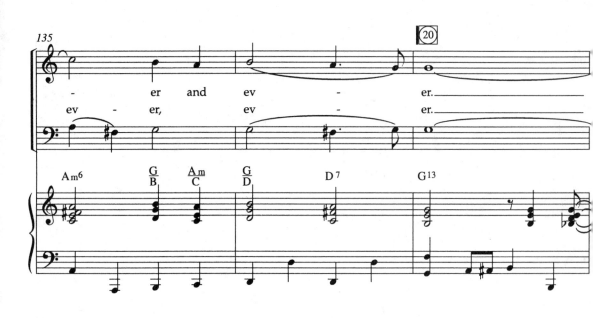

Silent Night

JOSEPH MOHR

FRANZ GRUBER
Arranged by Don Marsh

Angels We Have Heard on High
(From Company C)

Traditional French Carol
Additional lyrics by
Don and Lorie Marsh

Traditional French Carol
Arranged by Don Marsh

57

64

It Came upon the Midnight Clear

EDMUND H. SEARS

RICHARD STORRS WILLIS
Arranged by Don Marsh

Jingle Bells Medley

includes
Jingle Bells
Deck the Halls with Boughs of Holly
O Christmas Tree
Here We Come A'caroling

Arranged by Don Marsh

† Words and Music by JAMES PIERPONT.

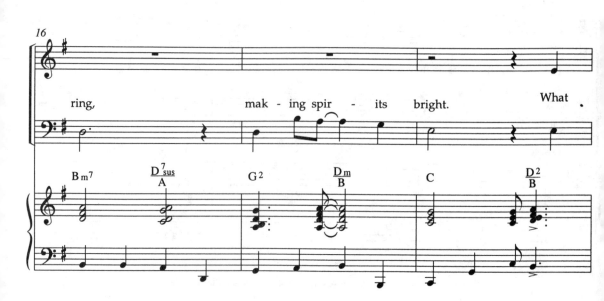

Oh, what fun__ it is to ride in a one - horse o - pen sleigh!__

†"Deck the Halls with Boughs of Holly"

Deck the halls__ with

†Words by J. P. McCASKEY; Music Ancient Welsh Melody.

-999984

† Words: st. 1 August Zarnack, Weisenbuch zu den Volksliedern fur Volksschulen, 1820 st. 2, 3 Ernst Anschutz, Leipzig 1824;
Music: Traditional German Carol.

† Words and Music Traditional English Carol.

*If girls are singing three parts, sing the top soprano note and the two cued notes.
**If the guys are singing two parts, sing the two cued notes.

We Three Kings

Words and Music by
JOHN HENRY HOPKINS, JR.
Arranged by Don Marsh

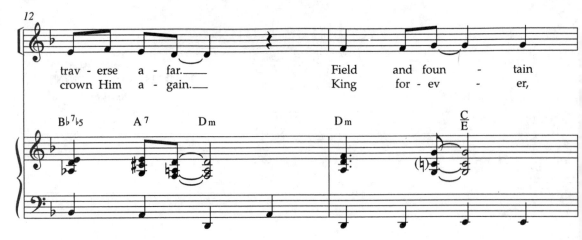

trav - erse a - far.___ Field and foun - tain
crown Him a - gain.___ King for - ev - er,

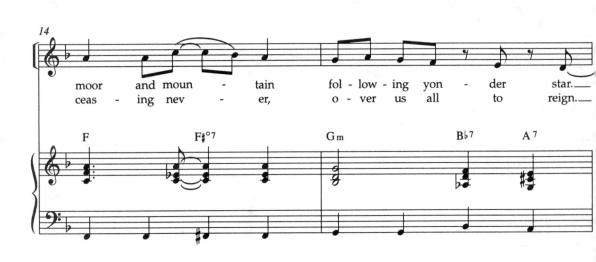

moor and moun - tain fol - low - ing yon - der star.___
ceas - ing nev - er, o - ver us all to reign.___

Both times: ALL
div.

Oh,___ star of won - der,

sealed in a stone cold tomb.

Oo

Am C7 B7 Em Em7 Em6 C/E Em

ALL
Glo - rious now ___ be -

Fm Ab Bb7 C7 Fm

hold Him a - rise ___ King and God ___ and

Db7b5 C7 Fm C7 Fm

come and guide__ us. Guide us to__ Thy per - fect

light,_____ per - fect light!_____

What Child Is This

WILLIAM CHATTERTON DIX
Additional lyrics by
Don and Lorie Marsh

Traditional English Carol
Arranged by Don Marsh

Joy to the World

ISAAC WATTS

GEORGE FREDERICK HANDEL
Arranged by Don Marsh

Joy to the world!

Joy to the world!